Special Tha

To everyone who had requested this book and nudged me into action!

To everyone who loves people and wants to make a difference, for showing me the wonders of their stories.

To my family and friends for their love, encouragement and support.

Jayne Thompson (Barny Books)
Dave Ricks (Light Up Creative Ltd)
Helen Peberdy
Anne Coles
Jane Lanverman
Deborah Hitt
Marion Wilkinson

Author's Note

Throughout my career and my life in general, I have been immensely grateful for this information and it really works for me and I hope it will work for you too.

I've written this book as the type of guide that I would have liked when I started working with people and wanted to do my very best to assist them with their health and well-being.

This book is set out how things relate according to the way I think, work and see things. When someone tells me about their symptoms, conditions, or illnesses, I do my best to make sense of their possible life situation so that I can be more understanding and more helpful in working with them

or being an aware friend. This relates to accidents, injuries and general life knocks (such as cuts and bruises) as well as emotional traumas.

Earlier in my life I may have ignored these signposts, however I've come to recognise that each and every one of us has our own coping mechanisms and strategies for managing and living life. Some people find it easier than others.

Maybe we are all actors and actresses hoping we know what we are doing, when in reality, our body is also speaking to us. Listening to these communications and honouring them in someone else is mighty helpful in being more understanding and even compassionate without making judgement.
All of my life I have been interested in the reasons behind people's ill health and conditions. There are a myriad of reasons why people get certain illnesses and diseases so it is wonderful to add the knowledge of what it may relate to, in order to glean the other potential emotional connections to situations. When I remember what some of the metaphysical and emotional reasons are, it is easier to be able to help   has their own way of learning and understanding.

I have presented the information and my opinions in this book in alphabetical order to make it easier to access.

You may want to look alphabetically in the book or use the index to find an area for parts of the body you are interested in. If you can't find the place you're looking for, then I suggest that you look for another way of describing that area or part of the body in the index e.g. colon / large intestine. It may help to look at something nearby e.g. if you want to know about the wrist there is information in 'arm' as well.

Foreword

Have you ever wondered if something in your life, other than physical factors, was having an adverse effect on your heath?

Over millennia, metaphysical mystery schools made a close study of this question, and codified the impact emotions, thoughts, events and issues in life could have on each part and function of the human body. Access to this body of knowledge was limited to the few. During the second half of the 20th century, some of this knowledge began to trickle out to the general public. It was of special interest to two groups of people, those wanting to take more control over their health and that of their families, and practitioners in the various fields of natural health.

Now, in first half of the 21st Century, Sue Ricks, in her most recent book, E–motion, takes this body of knowledge a step further. Respecting the unique complexity of each individual reader, rather than give one-size-fits-all affirmations or formulas, Sue empowers the reader with the highest gift, the gift of insight. She provides information related to each part and anatomical system of the body, for the reader to consider. We are invited to read, think about the information provided, explore and discover greater understanding within ourselves.

Natural health practitioners, with clients who have physical health problems that seem to never clear up, might find the insights in this book of substantial help. This E-motion book provides a wealth of information about what may be additional reasons behind client's present conditions.

On a personal note, reading and thinking about what is written in Sue's section on eyes, I've begun to look at some likely future adventures through different eyes.

In her personal lightness-of-being personality style, Sue combines previously obscure metaphysical information, along with her years of concentrated application of this body of knowledge, into this rich array of nuggets of information. It is clear, in this book, Sue's love and passion for all, to have a healthy, joyful, vibrant, deeply fulfilling life.

I unhesitatingly recommend *E-motion Energy in Motion* for anybody wanting to explore their own physical well-being as well as wanting to help family, friends, clients and patients to explore a little more deeply, other factors that might well be adversely impacting their quality of life.

Foreword by Bill Flocco

Bill Flocco has been specialising and teaching Reflexology and natural health since 1982. He is an expert in foot, hand and ear reflexology. He is a really dynamic teacher, school owner, author researcher, conference keynote speaker, organisational specialist and tireless advocate for the field of reflexology.

In my view Bill is one of the most respected reflexologists and educators in the world. He lives in California, USA and is head of the American Academy of Reflexology in Los Angeles. He is a much sought after teacher and presenter throughout the US and internationally.

I first met Bill at the Reflexology Association of America (RAA) conference in Denver in 2010. He comes across as the most sincere, honourable and immensely kind and loving man. His knowledge, integrity and passion for helping people is powerful to behold. I cheekily call him the 'grand daddy' of reflexology. I tell all my students about his work as he is a marvellous man to work with and so generous in his help of others. He is such a fun, wise and knowledgeable guy and I feel so lucky to know and have worked alongside him.

Introduction

There are numerous physical reasons for people's pain, inflammation or difficulty. These may be in a wide variety of different regions or areas of the body.

In this book I concentrate on the underlying emotional reasons behind potential problems, many of which affect different parts of the body.

When we recognise the different issues and aspects of life that can affect our health we take a big step forward towards potential health benefits. We cannot address things we don't know, however, we can make changes and take action or alter something if we know what may be causing health challenges or preventing good health. Increasing awareness, understanding and being open to potential reasons for health challenges means that these can potentially be addressed (or help sought) that positively impact on our overall health.

In this book I aim to highlight some of these aspects, themes and meanings in order to give the reader a clearer understanding of what may be going on 'behind the scenes' or aggravating, causing or adding to certain symptoms.

This information may be of value personally if you let your body do the talking and you are more likely to be able to pick up its messages.

"Our bodies communicate to us clearly and specifically, if we are willing to listen." ~ Shakti Gawain

It may also assist anyone who is working with others in helping to understand what may have previously been hidden messages or communication from the body. The more we know and understand, the more we can be proactive about how to care for ourselves, allow for our shortcomings and strengthen our best abilities.

A client came to see me with extreme pain in both of his knees. He said it had come on quite quickly and he could no longer kneel down as required in his job.

As part of our consultation I asked if he was under any stress at the moment and he told me that he was; his wife had asked for a divorce and that had come as a total shock to him. This all made sense to me as knees are about moving forward and are our shock absorbers. He had issues relating to both aspects, shock and moving forward hurt, in the same way as he said "my knees hurt", (You can read more about knees in the book).

By knowing more about what the emotional meanings of the specific part of the body are, it can give you more appreciation of the issues that they relate to.

Sometimes simply making the connections you can get more sense of what is going on when you know more about what the part of the body may be saying. The information is there if we pay attention to it.

Some years ago my friend was due to meet me for coffee and rang to cancel as she had hurt her back and could not drive. I went to her house instead and during our conversation I heard that there was talk of redundancies in the office where she worked. She had not been there that long and was worried that she might lose her job. She said she did not remember doing anything to injure her back and had just woken up with back pain. As I listened to her, I realised that her foundations had been rocked by the news of potential job losses and she was now feeling insecure about being able to provide financially for her son. This may be the likely trigger for her sudden onset back pain as low back pain is often associated with money worries (you can read more about backs in that section).

When we listen to our body or recognise what each part of the body may be telling us, it is easier to address the issues that are some of the underlying causes of illness and disease.

This book aims to highlight the ways to help everyone to gain better health.

A client came to see me complaining of shoulder pain, when I asked him if he was feeling a little overburdened by all his duties and responsibilities - he gave me a wry smile and agreed! When I explained about the meaning of shoulder pain as being about taking on the weight of the world, he agreed that this totally matched up to his current life situation. He was laughing as he told me how it had all started and how his life had changed since helping out a friend who was undertaking a big project. He said he had skills that he had willingly offered to his friend but recently had started to feel overwhelmed by the weight of responsibility he felt to make it a success. Everything related to the time of the onset of his shoulder pain and some of it was possibly due to what he was physically doing and some if it may be aggravated by the emotional pressures and feelings of overwhelm and responsibilities he was experiencing.

I hope you enjoy this book and get benefit from it, and realise how it can result in highlighting issues you didn't even realise were there.

Contents

E-motions Book

"Energy in Motion"

by Sue Ricks

Adrenals

Adrenals are about balance, dealing with shock, fear and anxiety.

They are associated with speed, a speedy life and the ability to respond immediately.

They can indicate the pace of life and whether it's all moving too fast.

The significance of the adrenals is that there are two of them situated above two kidneys and contain two cortexes. It is about the importance of pairing, working together and balance as in yin and yang.

Adrenal fatigue can be about life moving too fast and feeling disconnected, dealing with things in isolation (instead of being paired).

Keeping life in balance is key to healthy adrenal function as is paying attention to inner peace and emotional health. Over activity, overthinking or being too busy will stress the adrenals.

Because the adrenals sit on top of the kidneys they relate to connectedness to the higher aspects *(read about the kidneys on page 36)*, your values plus the natural flow of life. An issue with the adrenals could indicate that we have lost connection to the bigger picture. If it's all rush, rush, rush with no time to contemplate, enjoy and notice our quality of life, this causes stress and impairment of the adrenals.

Ankles

Ankles are related to digging your heels in. They actually hold the whole body weight which is an amazing feat as they are so small in comparison to the size of the rest of the body. They support the whole body and reflect inner and outer support.

Ankles relate to the ability to change direction and stand life forces (connecting the foot to the leg). Pain in the ankles can be when it's difficult to change or there is lack of support.

Swollen ankles indicate withheld emotion relating to lack of support or the flexible options available, whereas a sprained ankle indicates a strained time.

A flexible approach and attitude in life helps to increase flexible ankles.

Arms

Arms are how we reach out and offer. They are how we protect our hearts and communicate to others. Arms open wide are accepting, inviting and offering and yet arms closed across the chest are a protective measure.

They represent how we carry a load, how we can pull things in or push them away. We show our pleasure or displeasure with our arms. Issues with them can be about expressing inner feelings.

Reaching out and offering is done via the arms. Arms relate to relating and relationships. We offer with our arms and also receive too. It's giving and receiving in balance. Irritation and scratching of the arms (as well as self-harm) can be when someone is struggling with control or feeling lack of control. Stress can manifest as skin issues on the arms (plus scratching or picking). When there is too much to manage or control, the internal irritation may be experienced or seen on the skin on the arms.

Skin flare-ups can be experienced when our internal world and what we are offering / receiving is compromised.

Skin color – Red equals anger / embarrassment; white equals exhaustion, lack of energy; yellow equals fed up / cheesed off.

Arms can be affected by the need to control or the need to handle a situation. The more a person feels the need to take the responsibility for a situation, the more their arms may manifest weaknesses. If someone believes that it's up to them to cope with, handle or manage a situation - they may experience arm problems. Over control can be unsettling for others and 'dis-arms people'. People can feel disarmed when their coping strategies (management, handling or control) are compromised. It may be hard to reach out (their arms) to others for love, support and help and raising their arms in a request or gesture may feel like presenting a sign of weakness.

Arm – The top of the arm is governed by the throat chakra energy whose theme is communication. The bottom (underside) of the arm is governed by the heart chakra – love. Therefore, we communicate our love with all that (ideally) we touch and handle.

Our arms are all about giving and receiving; our wrists are about the direction of what we are handling; our hands are about what we handle, how we handle it plus how we handle ourselves and our lives; and our fingers are about the delicate fine tuning of life and how we handle our thoughts.

Hands relate to our careers and what we do in life - what we turn our hands to. Our role in life or career changes can impact on and cause hand pain or discomfort. Remember life phrases about idle hands relating to no purpose, intent or mission in life. Having a purpose helps with everything that is hand related however if there is too much pressure then hands physically experience the pressure and the pain too.

Sometimes the underlying message in society is that we are meant to handle everything, when in reality simplicity and reduction may be the resolution. If you have less to handle, it makes life so much easier and more pleasant.

Arteries

Arteries represent the flow of love through the body. The arteries receive oxygen – the breath of life – and move it around the body. Artery related issues are problems with 'going with' the loving flow of life, self and living. Blocked arteries can represent feeling blocked in with love; feeling blocked in with people and / or blocked in about life issues and aspects of life that the person does not love.

They reflect flexibility with going with the flow and generally love (or not) of life and what they are experiencing. The qualities of the arteries reflect real and deep feelings.

Back - (Also see spine)

Back pain can be due to too many pressures that compromise self-support. It is about things that we believe we have put behind us or maybe it is a need to 'push back' something or someone. Backs are about support and strength.

Upper back

Issues with the upper back relate to tension and to past events hindering the connection to love. It is the connection and integration area for the heart chakra and can relate to heart centred balance. Upper back issues can also relate to past hurts, fear, anger or low vibrational feelings i.e. shame, guilt and hate, (i.e. non love).

Love is the highest vibration therefore love, including love of self, is essential to resolving back issues.

Middle back

The middle back is difficult to reach physically and pain experienced here can relate to things that are difficult to reach or may be felt to be out of reach or impossible to reach or resolve. Pressures from society that are related to guilt, social pressures and things from the past can also manifest as pain in the thoracic / lumbar region.

Lower back

The spine and back relate to core issues, therefore pain in the lower back can relate to base issues of support which can include family, friends and finances (The 3 F's).

Pain in the lower back may also relate to money worries which can be about having it (or not) or keeping it!

Solutions can be creating base plans to be safe and secure.

Bladder

The bladder energy links to being fed up and is also directly linked to jealousy. When there is an apparent lack of personal power to make changes and alter whatever is making the person fed up, this may lead to bladder problems physical, practical or mental challenges (acceptance, If people can find acceptance or find ways round whatever the issue is, it helps the bladder to heal much faster).

The bladder is about fluid (water) and flow; it is about energy flowing freely. The kidney passes the fluid (urea / urine) to the bladder (chi flow) where it is held in the bladder and then released - this is the ideal flow pattern. The fluid gently flows in, is held and then flows out (ideally unseen). In Feng Shui there is a great deal of emphasis on the flow of water; how it moves, flows and leaves a house, garden or nature. Similarly it is important for the human body balance to maintain the same flow. Problems arise when someone is really fed up, when life does not flow gently; it may be moving too fast or too slow or be generally stuck. When someone has an issue with their bladder or urine it is very often at a time when something has made them feel pissed off.

The bladder is in the base chakra and so is related to something that is a base issue, about grounding, safety and practical reality.

The bladder is also about holding onto things and being unable to let go or letting go in an extreme fashion. Bladder retention problems are when someone is trying to hang onto their flow of life, when life does not feel flowing.

Bladder incontinence is when the general pressure of life is causing someone to be 'pissed off', fed up or when something needs to give under pressure. It is about venting dissatisfaction uncontrollably when the pressure of life gets too much.

Remember that water (urine) is about flow – too fast, lack of or painful.

Also water (urine) = fluid = emotion.

Emotion = energy in motion.

Question what type of energy is in motion? Is it in motion or stagnant. Is it flowing too slowly or too fast? Is it being withheld or rejected?

Being adequately hydrated, practising mindfulness, acceptance and relaxation will all help.

Blood pressure (High & Low)

High blood pressure is when there is high pressure on our life and what we love. These can be demands from and for loved ones, loved things and aspects or areas of life that we love.

Low blood pressure is when we have potentially given love all out and have not received (or kept) love back in equal quantities either due to lack of self-love, the over giving of love or the lack of loving being given back or received.

Blood pressure = pressure of love or loving.

Broken Bone

A broken bone indicates something has to give (break) or 'I might' (break). Check which bone has broken and what is the metaphysical (emotional) connection? i.e. a broken wrist might relate to handling an issue and something has to give. It is about having reached breaking point or feeling fractured on issues relating to the meaning of where the bone is broken.

Break + meaning of area where break is.

Breasts

Breasts are about nurturing, nourishment and mothering. They can relate to the care of self and others; maintaining a balance between over or under mothering is important.

Issues can be related to the over or under ability to take care of self and others.

These can be an overwhelming 'smother love' or possible denial of feminine aspects in order to nourish self. A person can feel under nurtured / nourished by life and circumstances.

Buttocks (bottom)

Buttocks / bottom relate to grounding and security. Lots of people store their insecurity in the buttocks / bottom / gluteal muscles. Relates to tension and the need to feel an element of control. The buttocks and bottom are involved in happily and successfully being able to go to the toilet (letting go). Buttocks relate to security, control and being able to let go (and relax). It relates to the ability to release old, used or no longer needed patterns, beliefs or concepts.

Chest

The chest is the place related to a sense of self. People beat their chest as a sign of power and the balance is linked to the feminine aspects of life and self-nurture. In men pains in the chest relate to their disconnection to the feminine aspects of self or sense of self. Pain in females is linked to the pain of connection to the female side of life (including expectations).

Central Nervous System (CNS)

The central nervous system (CNS) is exactly what it says it is. This is a central system that is central to us and our life and living. It's a system that works effectively or not!

It is an essential core system relating to nerves and being nervous. It's about anything that makes us nervous – central NERVOUS system! When anything or anyone gets on our nerves it can affect our nerves, nervousness or how we respond and react to things.

It is a mind / body connection in its purest form. The mind influences emotions and they affect the CNS and send signals from the brain throughout the body. It's a communication system about communication in all aspects of life.

Nervous breakdown. Information overload combined with no vital energy can lead to a nervous breakdown. Although it is extremely tough to experience or witness in others, it is actually potentially positive as the person's nervous system breaks down the way they lived before and a simple, more pure way (more true to themselves) is likely to evolve. It is a breakdown of the previous nervous system's responses and ideally a restructured, (less overloaded / overwhelmed) state occurs as they recover. A nervous breakdown happens if life is too much and too busy. So a breakdown is potentially good in the long term as it creates a more healthy way to live.

The CNS is our alarm and alert system. It transports messages throughout the body and the link between the brain and body is via the CNS. A person's body responds to various different stimuli however, what they are thinking has a massive impact of what the CNS has to deal with. One person can view life as being great with a glass half full whilst another will believe that their life is tough (as in the glass is half empty).

What we think about directly affects our moods, emotions and how our body responds. If it is highly tuned to be aware of contact threats (real or perceived) the person can be living on red alert when in fact life is actually fine. Much of this stems back to earlier life including childhood or any times of a big emotional situation or trauma.

The body responds to what the brain is saying so a person's thinking has a huge and direct effect on their body too. Their body is affected by the quality of their thoughts.

The CNS is like the earth matrix of the body. Everything is interconnected. All signals and messages are carried around the body. Some things are conscious whilst some are subconscious.

The nervous system is our body's primary communications

network. Our nerves, like wires, carry electrical signals or messages within and between all the parts of the body.

We have conscious or voluntary control over the sensory and motor systems of the central nervous system. The sensory branch of your central nervous system receives and transmits information from the outside world through the five senses (sound, sight, smell, taste and touch) to the brain. So, you can perceive the physical world around you while the motor branch of your central nervous system carries internal signals from your brain to your body, making it possible for you to walk, talk and perform actions in the world around you.

The autonomic branch of the nervous system is a non-conscious or involuntary system, which means that we have no apparent control over its function. The autonomic nervous system operates at a subconscious level to control all the functions of our internal organs and glands which secrete hormones.

Therefore some issues may be subconscious and ones we are not aware of. This is why therapy, self-development and awareness is so helpful and makes both emotional and physical benefits and changes.

Circulatory System

The circulatory system is the flow of blood (love) around the body. Blood is pumped by the heart and the theme of the heart is love, so blood is the chi (energy) flow of love.

The heart is a 'love pump' and circulatory issues are to do with loving or not loving life and the ability to truly love and be loved.

Loving and being loved are two very different elements of life. Some people are very loving but find it hard to accept and receive love (e.g. accepting compliments). Some people need to be loved but find it hard to truly and deeply love others. The ability to love and be loved is when great circulation can be most facilitated. The act of receiving reflexology or other therapy is an example of being loved and loving of self, enough to get help and support.

Poor circulation i.e. cold

If there is an issue with blood reaching the far extremities of a person's body then this indicates that love is not reaching and circulating through all areas of life and feelings. It may be that there is a belief that there is / was not enough love to go round, that they don't deserve love or that they receive it and give it straight out.

The more a person loves and is loved (and it's genuinely accepted and received) the better it is for heart energy and circulation in general. Some people love others and do not take care of or love their self. Love feeds the heart. It needs both giving and receiving in balance. The more we appreciate this the better it is for everyone.

Colon

The colon is linked to processing and discerning what the body (or person wants to keep or eject (reject). Also see Digestive System for a diagram of how the chakras are connected to understanding the colon and digestive system.

Ascending colon The ascending colon is about taking up life and beginning to process life. Starting with being grounded, being able to process, filter and digest and then by being ourselves creatively. It is beginning the process of digesting life.

Transverse colon The transverse colon is about honouring the 'me – ness of me', being creatively me, being courageous and able to cope with life shocks (or not!)and getting to grips with what is being processed about life or experiences. It is literally the gut speaking to us, hence the phrase 'Gut feeling'. The transverse colon area (sacral chakra) has a direct link and balances the brow chakra, which is intuition hence your intuition 'speaks' through your gut; Intuition = Brow chakra [link to] Sacral chakra = section of bowels.

Descending colon (also see the large intestine) The descending colon area is about staying grounded and being able to physically process situations, ideas etc while being able to let go of what is not helpful. The processing and letting go is not about generally accepted ways of living, but what is unique to this individual. It is about being the person that only they can be in the world. This relates to being able to make or create the final process (actions / steps / beliefs) and hence release unhelpful issues, patterns and thoughts. It is essentially a 'knowing what is right for me' space and about letting go or the inability to let go of other things, thoughts or aspects of life. Inflammatory diseases affecting the colon relate to a word I call 'shoulditis', i.e. 'I should do this or that'. Letting go of 'should' in your vocabulary will help enormously.

Diaphragm

The diaphragm is a massive muscle that separates the lungs (feelings) from the majority of the digestive system (processing). A strong and yet flexible person will follow their life's desires and the resulting action of the diaphragm will internally massage the higher and lower body cavities (chest and abdomen). If the person is experiencing a lack of heart's desire and is unable to process or know what's right or okay for them, the diaphragm can become tense and affect the higher and lower energies of the body both physically and emotionally.

Digestive system

The digestive system is all about 'How do I digest life?', 'How do I benefit from my life lessons?' As a whole, the digestive system represents how you digest life and make sense of it whilst working out what to do, how to cope, live and essentially be the real you.

We are fortunate to have the digestive system that is like a second brain plus a sensory awareness system. This provides us with access to our instincts as instinct (intuition) and gut are intrinsically linked. If we can listen to our 'gut instinct' and trust it, then this can save us much anguish. The digestive system is our internal knowing or guidance system.

Energetically the bowels (large and small intestines) are in three chakra and energy areas –

- solar plexus chakra

- sacral chakra

- root / base chakra

The function of the whole digestive system is to take in nourishment and process it. If you liken this to life – it represents how you take in life and how you filter and process life too. If there are digestive issues they represent the emotional problems and areas that require improving, resolving or learning about. Much of it is about awareness and family programming. Many people say that digestive issues are common in their family however it is important to remember that ways of thinking and behaviours are also passed down from generation to generation. We learn from an early age how to live, what to say or not say, how to act or not act etc.

Physically the digestive system is where the body takes what it needs and moves everything else on. In life this can be a healthy system or not. Some people know what is good for them and some do not. An example would be saying 'yes' when they mean 'no' and doing things they have to do rather than what they want to do.

When people resolve some of their 'should' issues and find ways that they can live as the person that they really are, their digestive issues may well improve.

My phrase for digestive issues is that it is all about 'shoulditis', a term I have used for many years to reflect the inflammatory nature of the condition! The word 'should' becoming like a disease (dis –ease).

Acid indigestion when life is caustic and things are stressful. Acid burns through things including our protection:

– the mucous linings of stomach etc. Acid is linked to anger.

– maybe because of having to do too much, doing what the person does not want to do or being the person they don't want to be. Not living the life they want can be when they produce high amounts of acid. More acid = more anger and or frustrations and dissatisfaction. Sometimes increased by having a high sugar intake and carbohydrates to satisfy the cravings for an easier nicer life.

Constipation – holding on very tightly! Cannot let go.

Diarrhoea – a rapid letting go 'oh shit!'. Everything has got to go!

Rectal prolapse – the world falling out of their bottom! Not really holding their own. It means a lack of grounding with safety.

Diverticulitis – pain in processing. There is no way out and things get stuck. When it is hard to live as the person (ideally) wants to, especially if there are requirements being imposed on them on how to live and how to behave. Pain is that processing.

Linking to Foot Reading

Ascending colon - in family and security (vertical zone). Questions - Can you be the person you really want to be? Do you understand you and your connection to the world? Do you feel lost at times and find yourself agreeing to things that you are not sure are good for you?

Is this a case of 'shoulditis' – 'I should do this' or 'I should do that' or behave / live like that.

Transverse colon – in the creativity and doing areas. Questions

- Are you really doing what you want? Are you living like you want - being creative at being you? Are you being a 'good girl or boy'? – however old you are!!

Descending colon – family and security – grounding and letting go.

Questions - Are you living and behaving as your family and society suggest you should?

Ears

The ears are about what and how you hear plus maintaining life balance. Many people are bombarded by noise and input especially as so many situations and experiences can create noise. This can be physical noise from external sources or internal noise created by the voice(s) in a person's head that is trying to make sense of the world, process life or handle a situation. Sometimes the noise is too much and they get ear problems.

Ears act as our antennae, like a radar to pick up signals from those around us. Ears pick up thoughts, vibrations and all sounds. Selected deafness is choosing what to hear and what to delete or filter out.

Ears are about what someone is hearing – do they like it or not? Have they heard it all before? Do they shut out the hustle and bustle of the noise of life by closing their ears to it all? Are they able to hear their inner voice? Is it okay to listen to their inner voice? Have they learnt at an early age that even though they can hear something and make sense of it, they need to follow their intuition in a different way – maybe they learnt not to trust it? Can they hear and trust their intuition?

Ears are also about balance. We have two ears (one either side of the head) and so they represent the balance of thoughts (we think in our head). The ears are how we physically keep our balance.

Ears are situated on the outside of the head and are therefore linked to thinking too. Recognizing the impact of our internal voice can help to reduce ear problems if the internal chatter is negative and can be addressed.

Eyes

Eyes are about our sight and how we see life, the world and our perception of life. Actual sight is how we perceive the world and our reality. They are our unique perception and personal view of the world.

Eyes = perception of life – how the person sees it.

How they view life, whether it is a good or tough life etc. People see things differently and eyes reflect that. Do they want to see (or not) a situation? One picture says a thousand words and everyone builds pictures of varying sorts in their head as a way of making sense of the world. One person's pictures may perceive a threat, problems and doom and gloom; whereas another person will see everything as a life opportunity, or about acceptance.

Endocrine System

The endocrine system in general relates to messages being sent and received plus the activation of a management role as this system affects many others and acts as a co-ordinator. If communication is hard, then it is hard for the messages to be received. The endocrine system may be living on red alert if the person is reacting to a continual stressful life and there may be too many messages for alerts being activated and trying to be processed. Their whole system can be overwhelmed leaving the endocrine system functioning in a chaotic fashion. Ideally, the endocrine system works in balance and harmony.

Hormones and hormonal activity relate to information and action in balance and manageable amounts – not too much or too little.

Excretory System

The excretory system relates to being able to let go and know what needs letting go of or what needs to be released in a balanced or appropriate fashion.How do I expel what I don't need anymore?

Face

The face relates to what and how we face things. Facing reality and expressing our inner thoughts that are revealed through facial expressions. Some people are facially expressive and are able to expand their energy to show in their face, others close themselves down as a safety measure and their face shows nothing (they've hidden deep inside themselves in order to protect their inner being). A bride's radiant face glows as an expression of love beaming from inside their being.

Acne – times of establishing own identity, problems with what is being projected out into the world.

Feet

Represent what you stand for, how to stand it and how you stand yourself. Feet are our connection to Mother Earth and how earthly and grounded we are. Any long-term issues may sink towards the feet (as in gravity), especially issues concerning guilt, grief or being overwhelmed.

Feet - Pale – not enough love to go round to get to the end of extremities. Holding onto vital supplies and love energy is depleted

Feet - Hot – lots and lots of (love) energy stored and ready to be given out into the world and express loving self into the world. Can be times of frustration and not being the true person they are.... Burning issues.

Feet - Cold – low (love) reserves so holding back love in order to take good care of self. When love reserves are full again then their feet will warm up. During a reflexology session the feet warm up as they receive the love through the self-care and connection to reflexology.

Toes - please see additional entry under the Toes section of the book

Fingers

Fingers relate to the activities and thoughts associated with what we are handling. The things that we are handling in our lives are our activities or jobs, our responsibilities or family demands and pressures etc. The digits are at the extremities of our hands and so they relate to things on the periphery of our existence. When we remember that the things that happen to us physically have actually begun in our levels of emotions or energy it shows that the fingertips connect us to, and are reflections of, the outer levels of our life and are super important to acknowledge.

In foot and hand reading each finger relates to a different aspect of our lives and living (see my book on the subject of foot and hand reading called Fantastic Feet, see page 65 for further information and detail)

- The thumb relates to thoughts
- The fore finger relates to feelings
- Middle finger relates to creativity and 'doings'
- Ring finger relates to communication
- Little finger relates to family and security

This can be followed through to demonstrate that the thumb relates to thoughts about what we are handling.

The forefinger relates to our feelings about what we are handling and so on.

The middle finger relates to what we are doing (or using creative approaches to) regarding what we are handling.

And so on for each finger.

Fingers and hands relate to what we are handling, how we are handling it and how we handle ourselves.

Anything that affects the fingers or one particular finger gives an insight into what may be affecting the person. Simply check which finger and look up its meaning and know it relates to that in regards to what they are handing (or not) in life plus how they are handling (or not) themselves.

It's fascinating. Every plaster or bandaid tells a story!

A blister means friction about whatever finger it is.

A cut means they are "cut up" about whatever the finger meaning is.

A bruise means they are emotionally bruised and the issue theme of that finger.

Gall Bladder

The gall bladder relates to issues to do with decisions and trouble with internal decision making. Gall bladder issues often happen when someone has to deal with a decision and they are 'chewing the fat'. The issue (decision) maybe about something that is unknown to others. The questioning is likely to be happening internally that others may not be aware of. Analysing options may be troublesome. Gall stones are fossilized decisions i.e. decisions that need to be made but have to be left for now. They symbolize something that's got stuck; no resolution, no obvious way out. Analytical qualities are required to process the decision and all options available. The gall bladder is governed by the solar plexus chakra and relates to the ability to cope with shocks, creativity and confidence.

Whilst writing this book I went into a shop and overheard a conversation between two people discussing the outcome of one of their pain and health challenges. The overheard conversation revealed that the issue had been resolved by having the gall bladder removed and the following comment highlighted the issue as they said, "and just when I am trying to work out what to do with my Mum and where are we going to live if the landlord terminates our lease?" Everything here is to do with decisions and the pain and difficulty of it all.

Remember 'emotion' means

Energy in motion

Fluid / water equals emotion involved

Emotion – e / motion

Energy in motion

Hair

Hair is the protector of our thoughts. Loss of hair can literally be an attempt to push thoughts out of our head. Extreme tension or trauma can affect the hair roots and cause baldness including alopecia.

The beard is related to strength and self-esteem and hair related protection. Dandruff is a blockage in self-cleaning mechanisms regarding thoughts.

Long hair is thought to enhance intuitive abilities.

Hands

Hands represent what you are handling in your life and how you handle whatever that is. They also represent how you handle yourself for example do you like and respect yourself or are you overly self critical etc?

The right hand represents the masculine aspects of life and relates to the yang, active, dominant and 'doings' side of life.

The left hand represents the feminine aspects of life and relates to the yin, passive, nurturing, yielding and self care sides of life.

Hands – Pale or cold – Insufficient love and warmth in what they are handling. This can be resolved by increasing the warmth and enjoyment of life (as in you get a warm feeling about whatever you are handling in life).

Hands – Hot or burning – means they have excessive amounts of energy stored up regarding what they are handling. It generally means that they have got too much on and feel stagnated or blocked in what they can do or how they self care. This can be resolved by taking small actions towards releasing the build up of pressure or energy regarding what needs to be handled.

Fingers - please see additional entry under the Fingers section of the book.

Wrists – please see additional entry under Wrists section of the book.

Head and Brain - (Also see skull)

Head = thoughts. Ideally they would be having peaceful and quiet thoughts, however it could be too much thought or worry. The head and the brain ideally represent our truth. The top of the head is the connection to the universe and higher connections. The forehead is being able to see and sense using the third eye (brow chakra).

Migraines – pain in our world. They relate to difficulty in seeing for lack of flow with the gentleness of life. It often means there is too little energy for self and thoughts of self-care. Occipital headaches – pain from the past that's unresolved. Possible forgiveness issues with something or someone in or from the past.

Headaches - pain of thoughts, doubt and lack of clarity, lack of self-awareness of what to do or how to be. Thoughts hurt = headache.

Heart - (also see circulation)

The theme of the heart is love. It is all about love and passions. It relates to feeling love, loving and what fills them with love. That can be people, situations, things, careers etc.

- For some people it is easier to love than be loved and for others it is easier to be loved than to love.

- Is it safe to love and be loved? – many have been deeply hurt and as a result fear loving and being loved due to past experiences including rejection and deep hurt.

The heart reflex can have grooves or deep lines across it indicating a past deep loss, grief or hurt (that may be healed by the giving and receiving of love). Multiple lines indicate several broken 'heart moments' that are now ideal for clients' own innate potential for healing via giving and receiving of love. Reflexology is ideal in these cases.

Wheel of heart balance

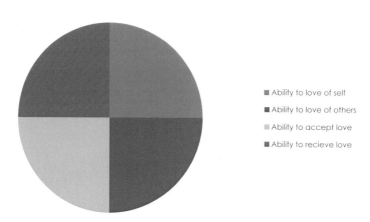

- Ability to love of self
- Ability to love of others
- Ability to accept love
- Ability to recieve love

Aiming for the ability to give and receive to self and others is optimum. True and deep love.

Hips

Hips are about the balance and pace of life. The flexibility of hips relate to the pace of life and the ability to be able to move forward. Is life moving too fast, does it need a real kick-start? Both things can have an impact on hips and the ability to support oneself in moving forward. Hip pain is linked to the pain of being stuck in a life situation and not being able to make a decision to change something; the lack of inner confidence to change and 'strut your stuff'. Hips give us the ability to pace out with strength and confidence.

Jaw (TMJ)

Jaw (TMJ Temporo Mandibular Joint - where the jaw bone meets the Temporal region of the skull) – the jaw is all about tension or relaxation. It is where we store our anxiety and can manifest as the tooth / teeth and jaw discomfort due to having to 'grit our teeth and get on with it'.

The TMJ represents skeletal (core self and strength) and energetic balance plus being physically and energetically in balance and in being your own person. The location of the jaw is a meeting point of the brow chakra energy and the throat chakra energy. The throat theme is communication and the brow is intuition, so it relates to communicating their intuition. When someone senses that this is 'not my way / not me' then they may clamp their jaw shut in an attempt to keep out other unwanted aspects or influences on life. It's about boundaries and maintaining barriers.

Tension in the jaw as you smile can be seen as 'grin and bear it' there may be no honesty in it - it's false and tense, as their smile represents skeletal (core self and strength) and energetic balance. Being physically and energetically in balance and in being your own person.

Kidneys

Kidneys are about filter and flow. The kidneys are the house of fear linked to all fright and flight issues which include anxiety, phobias and panic. Kidneys are about going with your natural flow and being able to filter out what is toxic to you what is helpful to you, to know the difference and honoring that.

The kidney's vital force (chi) is related to family patterns and anxieties in filtering what is helpful or unhelpful to an individual. The kidney is one of the most important organs of the body. The kidneys balance each other; the right kidney is the fire force (yang) whilst the left kidney is the water function (yin), ideally working in harmony together. If there is any anxiety or fear, one or both of the kidneys can be impaired in function. When kidney energy is low there is a risk to the whole body. If either fire (desire, passion and energy) or water (emotion and flow) are out of balance, then there can be a knock-on effect to the glomerulus (which is where the minute filtration process takes place).

In cases of overwhelm or anxiety there is thought to be a direct eye-kidney link and many diseases (dis-ease) of the kidney has an associated eye weakness as well. Family values and how a family 'sees' the world can be cascaded down the family ancestral line and result in kidney issues for a family member. Comments are often heard like "we don't do that", "we don't behave like that in our family", "it's not how our family does that" or "that type of thing does not happen in our family." These are seen as family values, traditions and beliefs but these can be individually challenged if they are unhealthy to an individual. When values are assessed, they can be retained if healthy or rejected if unhealthy. Retained equals holding on to, rejected equals released.

Knees

Knees give us the ability to bend down, to bow to life's pressures before standing tall again and the ability to move forward. Knees are our shock absorbers. They are linked to internal, gentle, quiet confidence with humility. Someone being brought to their knees is about having no energy and no power to move themselves forward. Knee pain is linked to issues (often fear) of moving forward and there is a link to kidney deficiency that affects knees (kidneys are the house of fear).

Large Intestine

An ability to let go of what is right for the person to know and discern what is good and what is not. Digesting life and digesting experiences and letting go. It is related to the ability to release and let go in a controlled manner. Some themes can impede the ability to let go including guilt from shame or regrets. Maybe part of the past is being retained and they may have a propensity to live in the past or be creating an imaginary future. Constipation is hanging on or hanging onto. Diarrhoea is "oh shit". To receive, there has to be space for the new to arrive. There has to be space to receive. In other words, release to receive. Ability to let go is important.

Legs

How we stand up for ourselves. How we run with the times. Support issues both practical and financial. Planning and maintaining support is important. Legs are linked to the ability to run with life.

Lips

The Lips are an amazing way of showing true feelings, as they are expressive and multipurpose. Lip problems occur when there is a problem with self-expression or expression of self (inner energy). Depletion of self can show as cold sores or painful blisters, etc. when there is less to smile about. Lips are used to smile and that uplifts moods. Babies and children smile much more that most adults!!

Liver

Characteristics of being judgmental, self-pitiful, experiencing guilt and shame, can get stored in the liver. Sometimes parenting and childhood patterns of how we should live get mixed up and cause illness, stress and angst. Anger, guilt and shame are common themes linked to liver function impairment. Not enough energy = lack of glycogen which is how we store and convert sugars for quick release. If we have no energy we can become angry due to feeling vulnerable with no energy reserves.

Liver – the liver is about storage and unprocessed emotions that hold someone back. As the liver is the biggest organ it stores the biggest emotions. These are often associated in needing bravery to be true to the self and can therefore be related to lacking courage or cowardice. It takes guts to be, think, behave and act as your authentic self.

It can be linked to characteristics of being judgmental, self-pitiful, experiencing guilt and shame, these can get stored in the liver. Very often there is a great deal of 'shoulds' that get caught up in the liver energy. This may stem from issues that relate to childhood, parenting issues and earlier times of anger, angst, guilt and shame. Often related to:

I should be different

I ought to cope better

It's related to having energy to cope – we store and release glucose – energy. Many times people feel they cannot cope as they use too much energy to be the person they are supposed to be and then don't have enough energy to cope. They get angry, feel guilty they cannot cope and react. Flare ups are a sign or depletion. Gentle courage is the positive attribute required.

Lungs

Lungs are all about personal feelings relating to freedom and space. This means the freedom to be ourselves and being able to feel safe in the space around us. Also the freedom to be who we genuinely are without the external pressures from life, others or society. Relaxed, deep breathing is much more likely when we feel relaxed and contented. Shallow, rapid breathing happens when we have a shallow connection to our true, authentic self and life is moving too fast. Lungs are our space and freedom to breathe.

In Feng Shui the room is seen as a lung - a living and breathing room. More breathing space as in having more room to live the way we want to live can help with lung issues. Stress of others can impinge on self and space for self and can have a knock on effect of influencing the freedom and flexibility of our lungs.

Lungs are like the tree of life. When you look at the lungs they are like a tree with a trunk, branches and even smaller branches (twigs). They need to be strong and flexible like a tree and well rooted in the ground. When someone is not well rooted in themselves and not grounded and feeling unsafe then their 'tree' can be unstable and the breath of life is hard to inhale so they need to inhale things that feed their essence (breath of life). Things like new ideas, concepts and life affirming intentions to create good feelings. They let go of what is not needed or has done its job (waste). It's about being able to receive and let go. Grief can be associated with lung issues too as there may have been something that has been unwillingly let go of or yet to release.

Breath holding is about holding onto control.

Rapid breathing is rapidly holding control when life is too fast. The respiratory system represents the outer world that is inside of us i.e. the lungs are inside the human body and are drawing in air (chi / life force) that comes from outside of us.

They represent boundaries in terms of drawing in the breath of life. In Chinese medicine, the lungs are paired with the colon; both give, receive and separate. They are part of the body's protection and defense mechanism.

The lung is the archetype of the father, meaning gaining self-value and the ability to leave home and find our place in the world whereas the spleen is the archetype of mother. Lung issues can be related to separation anxiety from mother or mother figures. Lung inefficiency can be about feeling lack of strength and personal power.

Lungs are about coping with feelings, enjoying life and being able to express self (so feelings are honoured).

Lymphatic System

The Lymphatic System represents our ability to get rid of what no longer serves us. The Lymphatic System is a little like looking at a map of the London underground where there are lots of stations (Lymph nodes) and train lines (vessels) where all the passengers may be either just passing through or dropping off their waste products as they travel.

The Lymphatic System is all about every kind of 'letting go', including letting go physically, emotionally, energetically or spiritually. Any fluid (lymph) that builds up represents withheld emotion (water equals emotion; e / motion equals energy in motion). What is the energy that is being held on to? (As opposed to processed and let go of). Lymph is moved due to some level of movement of muscles, if there is no movement, the lymph (chi / energy) stagnates.

Lymph problems equals chi / energy flow issues, no flow, or reduced flow. The area of the lymphatic fluid build-up will give more information of what the theme of their issue may be about. For example, swollen ankles equal withheld emotion and lack of flow to do with what a person stands for, how they stride out or forward. Lymphoedema in the arm can relate to what they are handling and carrying.

Mouth

The mouth is where we begin to break food down. It relates to the ability to break down ideas and concepts into bite size chunks. The opposite is overwhelmed and being highly emotional.

The mouth is how we take in nourishment. Problems with the mouth indicate a problem with taking in nourishment. It's where we chew things over (teeth), we speak our truth – or not. We take things in – food, air or reject (expel air or vomit).

The mouth and tongue is about speaking – speaking your truth, speaking out – or not. Are you speaking your values and beliefs or someone else's?

Neck

Holds your head (thoughts) up! Neck compression pain is caused by the weight of thoughts. Ability to turn the neck relates to the ability to see life in different views or directions and be able to make changes in life. Thoughts may be about reality, fears and projections or hopes and dreams. Bridging the gap between head and heart can change neck health. It is an extremely important head and heart connection that reveals a great deal. Pain in the neck can be related to someone who is being a pain in the neck. The neck relates to balance and communication when thoughts and emotions are in balance. Pain can be with thoughts and emotions at odds. A flexible neck means the person can look at issues and life in all kinds of directions and ways.

Nose

The nose relates to the clarity of space and smells of life around us. Blocked noses relate to feeling blocked in the way that life is faced and led. Sneezing relates to trying to eject the thoughts that run contrary to how life could be lived or addressed at soul intentional level. This happens frequently at times of disconnection from their true path whilst potentially living a 'should life'. Examples... I should do this, I should think like that. The internal mental pressures can cause extreme release by sneezing to eject the thought. Blockages can be eased by finding greater connection to your true path in life and living it. Love of the self in life increases immunity which also addresses allergies that can cause blocked sinuses and nose. Protection from life is part of the defense system alert mechanism.

The person's nose is in the middle of the face – so it's about what they are facing and related to breathing it in, how does it smell / sniff to them 'getting a whiff of…' , 'a sniff of something'.

Has someone or something really got up their nose? Is there a desire to sniff out something or maybe something does not smell right, as in feel / sense right. A phrase such as 'I got a whiff of an issue here' Do they sniff at that? Is there something that they are nosey about – want to know more about? Are they trying to nose around and get a sniff of where they are going or what to do next? What are they trying to nose out – discover / find / get at? In NLP there is a whole field of thought about people who process in different ways. The three most common ones are visual, auditory or kinesthetic, however olfactory (how it smells) and gustatory (how it tastes) are also significant. If someone is olfactory they will process by the smell of it all and this means they may be more susceptible to nose related issues as they sniff and smell their way through life. It is a sense and we need it, and for some it is greatly heightened.

The nose and mouth are the two ways that we inhale air and when the nose is blocked it stops us inhaling so maybe the breath of life is in short supply or is feeling blocked.

NOTE: multiple allergies relate to when people find it hard living here on earth. The challenges of the earthly plain can show up as allergies to things encountered in an earthly existence.

Ovaries / Testes

Ovaries and testes are about reproducing self. Do you want to replicate you? Is your life something you would like to replicate? It's about passing something forward for humanity to benefit by. If someone is unhappy with who they are and does not wish to replicate that or pass it forward, they are more likely to experience endocrine issues relating to the reproductive areas and this can be eased when someone finds more peace, love and acceptance for themselves and how they are.

It is also about knowing who they are free to be too and what they are here for or why. Sometimes we cannot even contemplate asking about replication of self as we do not even know who 'self' is!

Pancreas

Relates to the sweetness in life or a person could be too sweet for their own good. It might be about missing the sweetness in life. There may be an imbalance between being sweet and sour and swaying from one to another. It relates to the finer / sweeter things in life. There may be no fine or sweet things available or maybe they cannot be accepted or handled. Life situations could mean there is no access to the finer things or side of life.

Enzymes that the pancreas produce aid digestion and so this relates to the ability of the person to be able to break life down into small parcels / particles.

Sometimes life is not sweet or the sweetness is lost. Looking at the small particles of life can make it easier to find the sweet things (nice things or small aspects of life that are okay). An imbalance in the pancreas which leads to more challenges with blood sugar levels can be caused by someone receiving a shock of significant proportion or a sudden realisation that may be 'this is it!' And they don't like it.

Shock can impact the function of the pancreas and the physical knock-on effects can be picked up within two years of the shock occurring. The shock affects the solar plexus and that is linked to the islets of langerhans in the pancreas.

In foot reading, the pancreas is in the creative sector and in times of shock we may need to use all of our creative strengths to cope.

The pancreas relates to confidence, self-esteem and creativity. Shock can negatively impact all of these. The resolution is to take tiny steps forward to increase self-esteem, creativity and confidence. With an increase of all three of these, the person will have more energy, strength and ability to cope with any further life shocks. Being able to cope keeps the sweetness of life. Creatively keeping and re-finding or reconnecting with sweet moments is very empowering to anything pancreatic.

Pancreas – all about the sweetness of life (or not). Digesting life and creating the sweet balance of life.

Pineal

The pineal is something that anatomists know very little about however there are many factors that may help to explain about the pineal and what it relates to. It is thought to be part of our entry mechanism, i.e. how we arrive and join in with our body (between conception and around the time of our birth). It is the gateway to other realms. It atrophies over time and relates to keeping connection with the bigger picture. Our connection to our 'meaning of life.' As we 'arrive' (become fully integrated with our body) we do not need the pineal as much to help enter the body we are living in. As a baby we are still very much attached to our higher knowing (some call it 'knowing') as we get older we may lose some of these abilities and connections and the pineal shrinks accordingly.

Pituitary

The pituitary relates to our sixth sense. Our knowing of all that we know and yet may not know how we know! It is our internal radar and keeps us connected to our intuition. When the pituitary is working well and in balance, we find it easier to be connected to all of our senses and our intuition. We are better able to be guided on or with our potential destiny.

Reproductive System

The reproductive system relates to 'how do I keep myself safe and secure my ongoing line?'

The Reproductive System is related to grounding and replicating of self. Some reproductive / pelvic issues relate to when people are finding it hard or painful to be truly themselves, grounded or happy with themselves.

Life is full of 'meant to be' situations and experiences. However, some issues can be addressed or eased by looking at the bigger picture.

Questions like:

- "If you could truly be you, here on earth, who would you be? How would you be living, experiencing life?"

- "What changes do you need to make or could you make to be more of who you really are?"

Many people live in their head and so their energetic focus is very high - in other words, they are top heavy (energetically). An ideal situation would be that we are balanced with equal amounts of vibrant energy in our grounding (base) area and higher connection (crown) area. The grounding energy allows us to be rooted, grounded and who we truly are, and allows us to know how to live practically whilst feeling safe and secure.

Respiratory System - (Also See Lungs)

The Respiratory System is the system representing ability to receive (inhale - oxygen) and release (exhale – carbon dioxide). Another way of saying that is give and take. It is about the intake of life and abilities, practicalities and readiness to know what can be and needs to be let go of. The lungs are all about the breath of life and being able to live in harmony with giving and receiving.

Ribs

The ribs are our strength and protection for our lungs (feelings) and impose boundaries. We expand our ribs as we breathe (the breath of life). It's all about personal space. Ribs are a strong, boney structure that gives protection and movement to the internal (soft) organs. The movement and structure are key, if there is no movement or structure, the ribs may be uncomfortable. It's all about boundaries.

Scalp - (Also See Hair)

The scalp is the nearest body surface to our highest purpose. Scalp itchiness may indicate irritation regarding knowledge of higher purpose not being fulfilled or not knowing or sensing what it is. Scalp injuries may relate to times of feeling injured along your highest pathway in life (true reason for being here); feeling loss of or being knocked off course. Bruising or cutting (or banging) head may relate to times of thoughts occurring in the head when negative thoughts are being created. Therefore, missing the higher purpose connection.

Sensory System

The sensory system is all about connection to and being aware of their senses and feelings, inner sense, intuition and knowing.

Shins

Shins are associated with moving forward towards a stated goal. Problems and pain with shins can be related to times when life trips us up and prevents us from moving on.

Shoulders

Shoulders relate to the burdens, pressures and responsibilities of life. If the load of our lives is too much, the shoulders can bear the brunt of that and pain can ensue. A person may feel it's their role or job to just 'grin (TMJ jaw) and bear it (shoulders)'. Repeatedly being loaded with too much to cope with can weaken the shoulder's ability to heal and pain can follow in later life. Frozen shoulder or pain in the shoulder / joint capsule relates to being caught up in the load of coping with life. Fortunately moving on and letting go is the way forward. If there is too much responsibility to manage or bear their shoulders could become unbearable. If this inability or unwillingness to take on more has been going on for some time it can turn into a chronic problem. Discomfort can also be brought on quite suddenly if there is a request or a requirement to take on extra duties, tasks etc and there is an unwillingness i.e. the situation has become painful. Restricted movement in the shoulder relates to feeling restricted in life.

Pain in the shoulder region is related to the pain in shouldering life, responsibilities, projects, people etc.

If someone is unable to reach up due to shoulder pain or rigidity it means that they are finding it hard or painful to reach up to their highest values and concepts or live them (almost as if their life purpose is out of reach).

Sinuses

These are the cavities that make our head lighter (otherwise the skull would be way too heavy for the neck to hold). The very structure of the skull is extremely strong and thick in order to protect the delicate brain where we think and operate from. The sinuses are lined with mucus as a protection to the brain; some issues relate to negative thoughts that whirl round in our heads and the extra mucus produced is extra protection of the purity of being. Thoughts that roll around in the head relate to over production of mucus (to overprotect brain space). If the thoughts roll around and around with no way out or resolution (drainage) then sinus infection can be a result. Infected thoughts perpetuated in an ongoing cycle. A thought pattern that has a progression under resolution will help sinuses to drain.

Skeletal

The skeletal system is the core strength in us. It is the system that holds us up. How we hold our values and how we hold onto our life structure. If someone has their way of doing something and that is threatened, their core way of life is challenged and life can be painful = skeletal pain. Check the meaning of which part is affected and the metaphysical meaning for this area ie shoulder / hips etc.

This is life's structure - How are my life support systems? How easily do internal messages and my life flow?

Skin

Skin is the edge of 'me' and the start of everything else including 'you'.

Skin problems indicate how hard it is to be (or not to be) part of and integrate with the outside world as it is or 'appears to be'. The bigger the problem the more of a challenge it is to be here living in this world. A person with skin problems internal world is quite different to what they perceive it is like 'outside'.

The skin on the feet or body can reflect very similar things:-

Check where the skin issue is to be found on the body and then check the emotional connection meanings as well. If it's on the feet check the foot reading grids at the end of the book to see if there is any extra detail as to what the 'issue' could be relating to.

Acne or spots – indicates irritation and bringing issues to the surface and the need to resolve. If they keep coming back then look for further issues.

Athletes foot – can indicate infected thoughts and taking on other people's views.

Blisters – Extreme irritation that has actually reached the point of blistering. Fluid / blood blister – indicates irritation with withheld emotion. Burst blister – it's gone so far that it's now burst revealing the raw 'you'.

Boils – boiling up about something – remember to check where the boil is on the body to know what it may be about.

Bruises – bruised emotions; something hurts. They relate to thoughts that are hurting or even the time of life can hurt.

Burns – burning up about – a flash emotion happening quickly – a thought of annoyance or lack of self-thought / care time. Not being present and calm, burning up and marking time.

Corns – hard skin protecting a small and significant issue – (check grids on foot reading chart).

Cracked skin – cracking up about an issue. Cracked heels represent a split view on something that threatens the peace and security, which can often be family (outer family) related.

Cuts – Someone is cut up about 'X'. Check the meaning of the place or area that has been cut.

Dry skin – lack of nourishment, flow and smooth times. Can be withheld emotions.

Flaking skin – possibly shedding things to keep unwanted issues away.

Hard skin is protection - Check where the hard skin is on the feet or hand and relate to foot / hand reading grids to see where the extra protection is needed and has been created / retained.

Peeling skin – revealing the new you. Rough skin – having a rough time.

Warts – (inc plantar warts / verruca), represent a belief that is deep (it has 'roots') often thought to be a personal issue but is actually someone else's 'stuff'. It is a virus and has been taken on board by the person and taken on as in a belief or issue for themselves; it has been picked up, not rejected and is retained until it hopefully vanishes once a new belief is achieved!

The sensitivity of a specific area denotes sensitivity to a life issue in that area; for example, sunburn on the shoulders relates to burning up about responsibilities and burdens. Maybe because you are on holiday and wish for a carefree life but in reality they feel they have responsibilities to others to 'shoulder'.

Note: there can be some sensitivity if the person is actually more comfortable inside and likes privacy.

Accidents – some say it's a coincidence. Something happened by accident, however it may be a co-incidence, a mathematical term meaning 'the meeting of'. An accident may be just that or it may be 'meant to be'. Pay attention to wherever the 'accident' has impacted or affected and look up the meaning of that area, organ or part of the body.

Skull

The Skull is the structure that holds (contains) who we are here on earth. It is the casing of ourselves in our body. Head injuries may relate to times when it is traumatic, hard or painful to remain who we truly are.

The skull protects our thoughts and body management systems. There are 3 levels of thoughts

1. Thought – a brief and passing thought

2. Thinking – A cognitive process that we activate

3. Thunking (my word) – over thinking or repetitive thinking

Small Intestines - (Also See Colon)

These are about processing and problem solving; breaking things down to the smallest chunk helps to resolve the problem 'one bite at a time'. The daily grind (churning and processing of food) is related to the daily progress (or not) toward desires, aims and goals.

Solar Plexus

Our Solar Plexus is the centre of the emotions related to sense of self. It can also be known as 'Ki – bubbling spring.' It is the seat of self-energy, self-connection and inner confidence. A content Solar Plexus indicates quiet confidence, creativity and an ability to have a variety of ways of handling life.

Spine - (Also See Back)

The spine provides support and protection for the spinal cord and central nervous system – the spine is our core and central support – it relates to how we stand up to things, people and situations.

Upright versus uptight. Sacrum, the sacral area, mid-lower back, (grounding) relates to a special connectedness to Mother Earth; the support of life. Issues here may relate to the ability to acknowledge the support that there is, or the support that may be missing.

Lower spine issues relate to the biggest core worry that is often at the bottom of things for most people in the western world, - money worries – either getting it or keeping hold of it!

Spleen

The Spleen is a blood cleanser and nurturer. An earth based element that is about nurturing and replenishing. Problems with the spleen can be to do with family connections.

Stomach

The stomach is related to our ability to digest life and break it down into its smallest particles. There are links to creativity and ideas on processing life, ideas and concepts as in 'chew them over.' We roll off its concepts (around while we check it out, chew it over and move it on / forward). Ideally we receive daily nourishment rather than spurts. Stomach problems can be related to imbalance, excess, strength, and limitations. If someone 'can't stomach it' i.e. can't cope with a situation then they may develop stomach problems that reflect their discomfort.

It applies to an appetite for life and being able to stomach life. It is the first digestive organ and the start of the main processing of food being ingested (after the mouth). It is where the start of things is processed. A high appetite equals a high desire for life, low appetite equals little appetite for life (little is found that is appealing). Nervous stomach is when there is uncertainty or anxiety about going after true life's desires, i.e. what we really want. Improving anything about life makes it easier and more pleasant for the stomach.

The emotional scales help towards the next steps possible. See the chart at the end of the book and gauge current level of emotion and see what can be done to move towards a higher level. This may involve a change of thinking.

Stomach – how you stomach or cope with life and start to absorb and 'chew life over' – process started with chewing in the mouth. Stomach problems are when someone cannot 'stomach it'.

Teeth

Teeth – teeth are a way we chew food over and start our digesting process. If there are tooth problems these can relate to issues in life regarding what is happening and the way 'life is going'. Teeth start breaking through with babies as early as birth and continue through their developmental stages. Pain in the gums or the teeth can relate to a time when life is happening too fast and there is tension on assimilating and chewing it all over.

Some people do not chew their food at all and just 'swallow it whole' relating to just taking life and swallowing everything that comes their way. This is almost abdicating responsibility for the self. Chewing things over is a way of working things through. Over chewing things though can also be painful as there is too much 'chewing'.

Teeth grinding – anxiety and tension locked in (possibly subconscious worries in addition to known concerns). Relaxation, self-awareness and therapeutic intervention can really help.

Thighs

Thighs link the hips and knees. Issues can highlight a lack of self-confidence to access and use our personal power to stride out at our own pace and along our own path in life.

Thighs / hips allow us to swing and sway so represents movement (or lack of it) plus the ability to change direction or even dance through life.

Toes

Toes are the extremities of our feet and feet represent what we stand for, how we stand things and how we stand ourselves. The toes therefore relate to the fine detail of what you are thinking with regards to what you stand for.

The meaning of "stand for" is what is important to you, what your core beliefs are, what is most important to you and what do you value.

Each toe has a different meaning according to foot and hand reading, (see my book Fantastic Feet about foot and hand reading, see page 65 for further information and detail)

The big toe (hallux) relates to all things to do with thoughts. This is thoughts on what is thought about, reflections, inspiration, worries and thought patterns etc.

The second toe relates to feelings and how they affect our thoughts and also how our thoughts affect our feelings.

The next toe (3rd toe) relates to creativity and doings with regard to what we're doing and how we use creative approaches to life. It relates to how much we are being who we are (regarding what we stand for). Being us and being true to what we stand for is the essence of meaning for this toe (what's happening or not!).

The fourth toe relates to communication and that is on many levels.

Communication with ourselves, (internal chatter), communication with others and also our actions. The little toe relates to our family life and our security and how that affects us. Equally it relates to how what is happening (in terms of our security or our family) is affecting how we feel.

Tongue

The tongue is part of our communication and defence system. It allows us the ability to access and speak our truths. This ability to own true thoughts may be blocked by sugar coating and palatable truths, as salt and sugar are used to mask reality and make life more appealing.

Throat

The throat is another part of the head and heart connection. It may be linked to swallowing. It's a communication centre, a way of expressing emotions and feelings that can be stifled.

We use our throat to ingest food or speak out, using our vocal chords. It is about speaking your truth. Maybe voicing your truths or having someone else's thoughts 'rammed / shoved down your throat', can be 'eating your words.' An imbalance in honoring yourself and ability to voice this can cause tonsillitis, sore throats or laryngeal challenges. Throat infections relate to when a person's own voice has become infected by another's or society / family pressure or may be feeling pressurized to speak someone else's truth.

Coughing can be about a feeling that is blocked and causes an irritation or anxiety. Ideally express emotions freely.

Thyroid

The thyroid is the connection for the throat chakra and is our communication centre. It is all about checking technical detail (analysis) and digesting the world. Thyroid problems can be a head / heart disparity.

Uterus

A feminine expression of self. Ideas are nurtured before they are released into the world.

Varicose veins

Varicose veins occur where the veins involved in the venous return of deoxygenated blood are weak or this can be interpreted as the blood (love) flowing however we are then running out of energy to get the blood back to the heart centre and feed the self again. The oxygen has been transported but there is a weakness in the return to self. Giving out is okay however, giving to one's self is a weak system. Balance is the key!

Veins

Difficulty can show returning to old worn out patterns of love and self-care. Blood needs to be returned to the lungs and heart, via the veins, in order to be reoxygenated. Both arteries and veins need to be flexible and clear. Strength in love and life requires flexibility. Hardening of the arteries is about having to work hard and life is hard and inflexible. The more flexibility in life, the more flexible the arteries will be. Weaknesses in the arteries are covered by the human body with cholesterol, it's not always bad, to protect vulnerable areas.

Wrists

The wrists connect the hands (handling things) to the arms (reaching out / offering). When someone has issues with who they are and their right to give and receive, they may develop problems with their wrists. The wrist helps with handling and turning the hands in different directions. The ability to be able to use our hands is determined by the strength and flexibility of the wrist. When something new challenges or needs handling in a different way then the wrist may be painful until the problem is resolved. During pregnancy some women experience pain in their wrists through carpal tunnel syndrome as they have a new and potentially exciting yet daunting change to cope with, "How do I handle this?" "How does this affect me now?" "How does this change my life and my relationships?" "How do I cope and handle this?" "Am I ready or prepared to handle this?"

Emotional Scale

In order

- Feelings
- Love and appreciation
- Gratitude
- Passion
- Enthusiasm
- Optimism
- Contentment
- Hopeful
- Neutrality
- Boredom / Apathy
- Pride / Comparison
- Anger
- Craving
- Depression
- Guilt
- Shame
- Hate

High

Low

Bringing it all together

When you use this book to help you understand what some of the underpinning life issues could be, then you can look to address the situation as well as the ailment.

Sometimes people are unaware, living in blissful ignorance or maybe do not want (or are not ready) to know that their ailments are casued by emotional issues or situations that they find themselves in. These are my experiences about how things relate between body and life experiences, situations and personal life traits. We can either agree or disagree but what matters is doing the best we can for ourselves, those we love and also the world around us.

Being more aware of what the underlying issues are can help us be more understanding or get the appropriate help.

I see clients all the time in my complementary clinic and work with people over the internet and have witnessed the incredible power of people being able to change their lives so fast once they know.

One lady said that simply knowing that her crippling stomach pain (which medics could find no cause for) was probably exacerbated by the things she 'could not stomach' was a great relief. We spent a few sessions identifying what she 'could not stomach' and finding creative ways to overcome them. Within a month of her consultation with me she had radically (and very successfully) changed her viewpoint on some serious work stress, made great personal steps forward, been promoted and set a date for her wedding! She said that she now realised that her stomach pain had been alerting her to her pains in life which she could not 'stomach' and instead of trying to deal with them with pain relief medication, she would now listen and pay attention. One very happy lady!

I wish you love, enjoyment and fun as you help yourself, those you love and anyone this is appropriate for.

Energy follows thought so let's think good thoughts about life, living and love.

Sue x

Chakra
Key Points

Crown Chakra

Action:	Spiritual / Higher Self connection Wisdom / Peace Purpose
Endocrine Link:	Pineal
Colour:	Purple

Brow Chakra

Action:	Intuition / Inner Vision Perception / Inspiration Synchronicity / Reflection
Endocrine Link:	Pituitary
Colour:	Indigo

Throat Chakra

Action:	Communication Self expression Personal Truth Authenticity
Endocrine Link:	Thyroid
Colour:	Blue

Heart Chakra

Action:	Love / Passion Compassion / Integration Self Love / Awareness Rejuvenation
Endocrine Link:	Thymus
Colour:	Green / Pink

Solar Plexus Chakra

Action:	Self Esteem / Problem Solving / Confidence / Responsibility / Ability to cope with shocks
Endocrine Link:	Pancreas
Colour:	Yellow

Sacral Chakra

Action:	Creativity / Processing / Discernment / Emotions Sexuality / Freedom
Endocrine Link:	Adrenals
Colour:	Oranges

Base / Root Chakra

Action:	Grounding / Self preservation / Practicality / Reality / Safety / Stability / Trust
Endocrine Link:	Reproductive Organs
Colour:	Red

suericks.com

Chakra
Key Points

Crown Chakra

Action:	Spiritual / Higher Self connection Wisdom / Peace Purpose
Endocrine Link:	Pineal
Colour:	Purple

Brow Chakra

Action:	Intuition / Inner Vision Perception / Inspiration Synchronicity / Reflection
Endocrine Link:	Pituitary
Colour:	Indigo

Throat Chakra

Action:	Communication Self expression Personal Truth Authenticity
Endocrine Link:	Thyroid
Colour:	Blue

Heart Chakra

Action:	Love / Passion Compession / Integration Self Love / Awareness Rejovenation
Endocrine Link:	Thymus
Colour:	Green / Pink

Solar Plexus Chakra

Action:	Self Esteem / Problem Solving / Confidence / Responsibility / Ability to cope with shocks
Endocrine Link:	Pancreas
Colour:	Yellow

Sacral Chakra

Action:	Creativity / Processing / Discernment / Emotions Sexuality / Freedom
Endocrine Link:	Adrenals
Colour:	Oranges

Base / Root Chakra

Action:	Grounding / Self preservation / Practicality / Reality / Safety / Stability / Trust
Endocrine Link:	Reproductive Organs
Colour:	Red

suericks.com

Foot Reading Meanings Grid

Thoughts

Feelings

Creativity & Doing

Communications

Family & Security

www.suericks.com

Want to Know More?

If you have enjoyed this book, you may find my other books & DVD's useful too. These are all available through www.suericks.com

My first book, "**Three Steps To Enjoying Life**", is what I call my traveling book as one copy goes from friend to friend or from person to person.
It is a quick and easy read on how to enjoy life even more.

My second book is "**The Gentle Touch of Reflexology for Babies and Children**" and focuses on Reflexology techniques that you can use for the younger generation. It is full of easy to follow techniques, advice, hints and tips. It includes full colour images, diagrams and charts.

My third book is "**Fantastic Feet**" providing real photographs with details of foot and hand reading. Also how to link into the emotions.

My DVD's are:

- **DVD 1 – Gentle Touch Reflexology**. This includes 1 1/2 Hours of tuition on the use and practical application of Gentle Touch Reflexology.
  It is a close up guide to the techniques.

- **DVD 2 – Gentle Touch Reflexology - Advanced Techniques**.
  It includes 16 additional advanced techniques that you can use to assist people using Gentle Touch Reflexology.

- **DVD 3 – Success Tips for Reflexologists**. Full of helpful advice and creating increased opportunities for a happy, healthy and successful career in Reflexology.

- **DVD 4 – Everyday Techniques**. A guide for all on how to stay strong safe and happy. Four essential techniques are suitable for all and can be used anywhere including office, home and life in general.
  Life enhancing.

- **Reflexology for Babies and Children DVD 1 & DVD 2**. Extensive information including practical techniques, advice and guidance on using Reflexology for the younger generation.

There are also a range of charts and other products available.

For more information

www.suericks.com